Baby Animals
KITTEN

Angela Royston

Chrysalis Education

Distributed in the United States by
Smart Apple Media
2140 Howard Drive West
North Mankato, Minnesota 56003

Library of Congress Control Number: 2003070054

ISBN 1-59389-158-X

Editorial Manager: Joyce Bentley
Project Editors: Lionel Bender and Clare Lewis
Designer: Ben White
Production: Kim Richardson
Picture Researcher: Cathy Stastny
Cover Make-up: Mike Pilley, Radius

Produced by Bender Richardson White, U.K.

Printed in China

10 9 8 7 6 5 4 3 2 1

Words in **bold** can be found in New words on page 31.

NOTE
In this book, we have used photographs of different types of kittens and adult cats. Each type has fur of a certain color and pattern.

Picture credits
Chrysalis Images/Jane Burton: 18, 24.
Corbis Images Inc: Michael Busselle 9; Pat Doyle 17.
Ecoscene: Robert Pickett 15, 28; Angela Hampton 21.
Lionheart Books: 2, 22, 29.
Natural History Photo Agency: Jane Knight 26.
Rex Features Ltd: David Hurrell 27.
RSPCA Photolibrary: E A Janes cover, 25; Geoff de Feu 23; John Downer/Wild Images 6, 8, 11, 13;
Angela Hampton 1, 4, 5, 7, 10, 12, 14, 16, 19, 20, 25.

Contents

Just born

These tiny kittens have just been born. Their **fur** is all wet.

The mother cat licks the kittens. Soon their fur is dry and fluffy.

A few hours old

The newborn kittens cannot see or hear. They stay close to their mother.

Even when a newborn kitten is awake, its eyes are always tightly shut.

Feeding

This newborn kitten is hungry. She sucks milk from one of her mother's **teats**.

Kittens usually feed together.
After they have taken milk,
they will go back to sleep.

A few days old

The kittens spend more time awake now. They begin to crawl around the floor.

The mother cat looks after the
kittens. If one strays too far, she
carries it back.

Two weeks old

These kittens have just opened their eyes for the first time. Now they can see!

The kittens' ears are working, too. They can hear their mother **miaowing**.

Four weeks old

The kittens are growing bigger and stronger. They start to run around and play.

They now spend more time
on their own, away from
their mother.

Six weeks old

Kittens love to **explore**. They climb into bags and boxes.

They smell everything they find.
They are very curious.

Playing

Kittens love to play. They **claw** at objects and pretend to fight with each other.

Sometimes they **nip** each other
and roll around the floor.

Nine weeks old

The kittens no longer feed on their mother's milk. Instead they lap up water.

They eat special cat food. They each have their own saucer or share a large dish.

Twelve weeks old

The kittens are now old enough to go outside. At first, they are nervous.

This kitten has climbed into a tree. When it jumps down, it always lands on all four feet.

Learning to hunt

Kittens love to **paw** and chase anything that moves.

The kitten watches and then **pounces**. He is practicing how to **hunt** mice.

Keeping clean

The kittens learn how to keep themselves clean. They use their tongues to clean their fur.

This kitten is cleaning her face. She licks her paw and then rubs it over her face.

One year old

Each kitten grows bigger and bigger until it becomes an **adult** cat.

Grown-up cats still like to play and explore, but they also like to rest in the sun.

Quiz

1 Can a kitten see or hear when it is first born?

2 How old are the kittens when they first open their eyes?

3 Do kittens like to play with one another?

4 When do kittens stop feeding on their mother's milk?

5 What sound does a mother cat make to call her kittens?

6 At what age can kittens safely go outside?

7 How old are kittens when they are fully grown?

8 How do cats clean their fur?

The answers are all in this book!

New words

adult fully grown—a grown up.

claw long, curved, sharp toenail on a cat's foot; to scratch, scrape, or dig with claws.

explore to find out for oneself.

fur thick hair that covers most of the kitten or cat's body.

hunt look for something, particularly for food.

miaow the noise that a cat makes, usually when it wants something.

nip a small bite.

paw foot; to touch or strike with a paw.

pounce jump or leap on something from a height.

teat part of a mother's body from which her babies suck milk.

Index